Politics:
Easy as P.I.E.

Bob McEwen

First Printing   2003
Second Printing   2004
Third Printing   2005
Fourth Printing   2006
Fifth Printing   2007

CONTENTS

INTRODUCTION

Have you ever wondered why some people are rich, while others seem to struggle financially?

Have you ever wondered why some nations' docks are filled with cargo, their stores brimming with goods, while other nations are filled with starving people, abandoned stores and empty shelves?

Well, there are a few fundamental principles that, when understood, bring prosperity, but if ignored, bring poverty. They are the indispensable ingredients of wealth.

While these principles are not complicated, they are very important. This book will identify and explain these principles.

Fundamentally, the wealth of a nation and the resulting prosperity of its citizens hinges upon one thing: its politics.

"But I don't understand politics, and besides, I'm not really very interested." If these are thoughts you share, then you have come to the right place, for you will discover that understanding is as "easy as P.I.E.!" And once you understand, you will care.

As you will soon see in the pages that follow, politics is simply a question of whether decisions are made for people, or whether people are allowed to make decisions for themselves. We make that choice when we cast our ballot.

Thus, we select our political leaders on primarily two criteria: integrity and economics. That is, the politician's integrity and his economic philosophy. Hence, the formula:

Politics = Integrity + Economics

or

P. = I. + E.

Just as a finished apple pie is a melding together of simple parts, so too is politics. Here's the difference: While I won't promise to teach you how to make a great apple pie, I will promise to teach you how to intelligently and responsibly participate in politics.

After all, as citizens who are empowered with the privilege of electing our political leaders, we are ultimately accountable for the success or failure, wealth or poverty of our country. If we wish to pass to future generations a free country with its riches and power intact, we must choose leaders who will protect freedom and build prosperity. Let us learn how to do just that.

CHAPTER ONE: POLITICS

"BUT I DON'T UNDERSTAND

THE LABELS!"

Principle: The higher the taxes, the greater the government's control.

Impact: The more money that is taken away from you through taxes, the more limited are your individual choices.

Explanation: Thomas Jefferson once said that "Freedom is having choices." When the government takes your money through taxes, it reduces your choices, thereby reducing your freedom.

The labels "Free Enterprise" and "Socialism" merely identify whether a country or an individual is in support of more or less freedom. While these may be terms that you cannot currently define, they are concepts that you currently know. That is, there are only two basic economic ideas, and you already understand them both.

THE POLITICAL YARDSTICK

Picture, if you will, a large yardstick. On one side, all the way to the left, is government control of the tools of production. In other words, the government controls the businesses.

On the far right is complete freedom. The government takes nothing. You can own anything you want to own, earn anything you want to earn. You get to keep it all.

> **ECONOMIC IDEA #1:**
>
> **Socialism is government control of the tools of production.**

Along the gamut of this imaginary yardstick, you will find all of the various governments throughout the world. Those on the far left are Socialist. In countries such as North Korea and Vietnam, the government controls everything. We should note that it is not a coincidence that all of the countries on the far left are also the poorest countries in the world.

As you move along this virtual yardstick towards the right, the wealth of the nations increases. As we will see, the more freedom citizens have from government control, the greater the wealth of the nation.

On the far right we find pure Free Enterprise. Here, a person may wake up in the morning and decide to sell his hog. He finds a willing buyer, they agree on the price, and he sells his hog. All of this is done without a government official being involved.

> **ECONOMIC IDEA #2:**
>
> *Free Enterprise is enterprise free of government interference*

In other words, Free Enterprise is the natural order of things. It is a willing buyer and a willing seller freely engaging in the transaction of a business enterprise. Thus, the term "Free Enterprise." It is enterprise free of government interference.

Of course, very few transactions are completely independent of the government. After all, government money makes the exchange work more smoothly. So, perfect free enterprise is rare.

On the other hand, only in a prison does the government control all exchanges, so pure Socialism is also rare.

As a result, the economic environment in which we work is somewhere on this spectrum between Free Enterprise and Socialism. Political elections are the tool we use to decide where on that spectrum you and I will live. Over the next few pages, you will be able to judge for yourself which system you prefer.

Over the next few pages, you will be able to judge for yourself which system you prefer.

OUR NUMBER OF CHOICES DETERMINE THE EXTENT OF OUR FREEDOM

Let us return to our principle: **the higher the taxes, the greater the government's control**. And remember, the greater the government's control, the fewer the choices.

The best rule of thumb to judge where a nation falls on the political yardstick is to look at its overall tax rate. The question is, how much of all that is produced in a country is taken by the government? As you may well have guessed, those governments on the left of the political yardstick take the most; those on the right take the least.

In the United States, up until the 1950's, we were at the 20% mark. That is, government took 20% of a person's income. People put 80% of what they earned into their pocket.

Today, we are at the 40% mark – just about 40% of everything we make goes to the government, and we put the other sixty percent in our pocket. While we are still on the side of freedom, we have spent the last several decades inching ever closer to the side of Socialism.

And so, over the course of every election, you and I very simply do this: We decide whether or not to move that scale towards tyranny and government control, or towards Free Enterprise.

There is a widely told story of a frog in a pot. As the story goes, if you put a frog into a pot of boiling water, it will immediately sense danger and it will jump out. However, if you place this same frog in a pot of room temperature water and then place the pot over a flame, the frog will contentedly sit in the pot until it boils to death. The moral of the story? The frog only recognized a threat to its survival if the threat was violently abrupt.

It is no different for you and me and the freedom we enjoy as Americans. It is for this reason that the framers of the Constitution warned us of the discreet threats to our liberties. "I believe there are more instances of the abridgement of the freedom of the people by gradual and silent encroachments of those in power than by violent and sudden usurpations." Such were the words of James Madison at the 1788 Virginia Ratification Convention. Such is the threat we face today.

In a free country such as ours, the gradual and silent encroachments to our liberties - the ever warming water - come in the form of taxes.

"How does that happen?," you ask. Let us suppose that after a full week's work, you are given your just pay. You have earned $100.00. Now, there are only two people that can take this money away from you. The first is a criminal. A criminal may have a gun and take some or all of your money, thereby reducing your choices as to how you will use that $100.00.

The second is the government. It also has a gun and can take your money away from you. It also infringes upon our freedom of choice. The result? Fewer choices, less freedom and ultimately, a lower standard of living.

UNCLE SAM: OUR SILENT PARTNER

The typical family in the 1950's consisted of a husband who went off to work every day and supported the family, and a wife who filled the vital role of homemaker.

In the 2000's, the typical family consists of two working spouses who, combined, earn barely enough to make ends meet. The woman tends to make less than the man. She generally contributes 40% to the household, while he contributes 60%. Coincidentally, the tax rate in the U.S. is roughly 40%. As a result, a woman will work an entire year and at the end of the year, what will she have to show for her dedication and effort? In effect, she will place every penny she earns into Uncle Sam's coffers. She will work an entire year to fund the many government programs which, in their inception sound wonderful, but in their implementation require more taxes to make them work.

OUR FREEDOM OF CHOICE DETERMINES OUR STANDARD OF LIVING

Think of a menu in a restaurant. Suppose that the most expensive item on the menu costs $50.00 and you have a $50.00 bill in your pocket. You have complete freedom to choose anything on the menu. Your choices are unlimited.

Now let us assume that either a criminal or the government takes $10.00 away from you. There will now be some items on the menu that you can no longer afford. Assume $30.00 was taken from you, leaving you with only $20.00 – fewer choices still.

What has happened? Your freedom has been restricted. Though you would like to choose the $50.00 item on the menu, you cannot. Try though you might, you cannot increase the quality of the meal you will receive because your choices have been limited by the government.

While you may not be distraught over the loss of choices on a menu, the principle applies in all areas. If money is taken away from you, your loss of choices results in a lower standard of living. The size home in which you live, the kind of car you drive, the length of vacation you can take – all of these are directly related to your income and how much of it you are allowed to keep.

Thus, we see that your standard of living is directly impacted when either the government or the force of a criminal element takes your money from you.

It naturally follows that whenever a politician uses the police powers of the state to take money away from you, you are left with fewer choices and a lower standard of living. Conversely, the more money that people are permitted to keep, the greater amount of choices, the greater their freedom, and ultimately, the higher their standard of living.

One government tilts toward the right of the political yardstick, conferring on its citizens the freedom of choice to increase their standard of living.

THE SHIFTING STANDARD OF LIVING

In the 1950's, the typical American family rarely ate out – it was considered an activity in which only the rich regularly participated. The typical family had one television and one telephone – it was black and sat in the middle of the home. Rarely did the typical family purchase a new vehicle. If someone did, it was a novelty item for all in the neighborhood to inspect. Air conditioned homes were rare and air conditioned cars were virtually non-existent.

The standard of living in America is ever-shifting. Today, the average person in America who is on welfare nets $2000 per year more in equivalent dollars than did the average family in 1950. No country in the world has a greater standard of living than do we Americans. Western Europe is the closest, and the average resident of Western Europe lives on less square footage, is less likely to have a telephone or air conditioning, than the average American on welfare, who by our definition is considered poverty-stricken!

One government tilts towards the left of the political yardstick, restricting its citizens' freedom to choose a greater standard of living and in fact foisting upon them a low standard of living.

As we discussed earlier, it is up to you and me to choose which system we prefer. It is up to you and me to protect that system when we cast our vote.

RECOGNIZING THE LABELS

Since people do not walk around with signs that say "Free Enterpriser" or "Socialist" on them, it is important that we learn to recognize a person's belief system through his words. Now that you know what the characteristics of each system are, you will for the rest of your life be able to recognize that, "This person thinks like me," or "This person thinks in a way that I believe is destructive to our system."

When you hear a politician promoting free housing and universal medical care, you will immediately know that he is in inclined towards government control. When you hear a politician speak of lower taxes and warn against "big government," you will immediately know that this person favors Free Enterprise.

Thus, the left side will always want more taxes; the right side will always want less. The left side believes government should have its hand in health care, utilities, and the operations of private industry. Fundamentally, the left believes that the government is more capable of making the best decisions for people than are the people themselves.

The right believes the opposite. They believe that government should only do that which we cannot do for ourselves. The right looks to the Declaration of Independence for the government's authority: "For this cause governments are instituted upon men ... for the preservation of life, liberty and the pursuit of happiness." The right therefore only supports taxation for activities that meet this standard, such as the development of a strong national defense to preserve our liberty.

We could continue with example after example, but here is the point: once you understand the two radically different ways of thinking, you can assess whether the politics that a particular candidate advocates will lead our country towards Socialism, or towards Free Enterprise. As was mentioned just a few short moments ago, you must determine which system you prefer.

CHAPTER TWO: ECONOMICS

"WHY DO SOME POLITICIANS MAKE THEIR CITIES AND NATIONS POOR?"

Principle: The greater the freedom, the greater the wealth.

Impact: The more a country attempts to distribute wealth through government control, the more impoverished the country will become.

Explanation: In addition to believing that government must make decisions for people because people are inherently incapable of making decisions for themselves, the left also believes that there is a set amount of wealth. They therefore favor government control and believe that it is up to the government to distribute it so that everyone can share it fairly.

Here is the problem. **If you have a fundamental failing in your understanding, you will come to wrong conclusions.** If you think you can get to Los Angeles from Memphis by driving East, no matter how fast you go, you will not get there because you have just such a fundamental misunderstanding.

The people on the left have a fundamental misunderstanding about wealth. They do not understand that there is no set amount of wealth. They do not understand that wealth comes when free people under free enterprise *create*. They *create* a fax machine, *create* a telephone, *create* all of the wealth that in and of itself, whether it be coal or iron or steel, has no value. This is why the former Soviet Union was number two in the *world* in gold but was dreadfully poor. They had the resources. They did not have the freedom.

> *Only in a free system are people able to create wealth*

Only under freedom are people able to *create* wealth. The right never fears poverty because they know that whatever they encounter, they can always *create* more. The left truly do not know how to *create*, so they are in constant fear of running out of what they currently see, because they believe there is nothing that can be done about its depletion.

Just as you can identify a person's political philosophy through his words, so too can you identify his understanding of wealth. Those who fret endlessly that we are going to overpopulate or run out of energy do not understand wealth. They do not understand that a country's wealth comes from *innovation* and that it is *unlimited*.

THE ECONOMY

Let us examine wealth in the context of the economy. The dictionary defines economics as "the social science concerned with the production, distribution, and concerned of goods and services." It is all of the stuff that we buy and sell in the whole country. The sum total of everything that is bought and sold is the country's economy.

Thus, if the news reports that we are experiencing an economic slump, it means that we are buying and selling fewer things. An economic upturn would be just the opposite. It's people buying and selling more things.

This ties in directly with what we discussed in the last chapter. Remember the menu? The more money we have, the more choices. The more money we have, the more things we can buy. The more money we have, the better our economy.

Most importantly, a vibrant economy is the one that allows free people to be free to create ways for us to do things that were previously impossible.

Have you ever wondered why America is the richest, most powerful nation on earth? It isn't that we work harder or that we're smarter. It isn't by accident that we create every year more inventions than the rest of the world combined. It isn't by accident that we have won more Nobel peace prizes than the rest of the world combined. We create more jobs, more music, more books, more community plays, and more symphonies than the rest of the world combined, because we have the most freedom to do so. Remember our principle: **The more freedom, the more wealth.**

THIRD PARTY PURCHASING

There is also more abundance in a free society because there is far less waste. For example, let us suppose that tomorrow afternoon you go to buy something for yourself. You care about two things – price and quality. In a restaurant, you scrutinize the menu and assess your hunger; you wonder whether the entrée

> *There is also more abundance in a free society because there is far less waste.*

is worth nine or ten dollars. You may look at a car or even a bottle of water and evaluate how cold, how pure it is. You make all of those judgments about the price and the quality of an object and when those two meet, you purchase it.

But let us suppose that you are not buying something for yourself. You are in fact buying it for someone else. Since you are still paying for it, you care very much about the price. But you are a little more flexible on the quality. You think to yourself, "Mustard yellow? Yeah, she'll like it!" We have all done it. We have all purchased things that we would not have bought for ourselves. We cared about the price, but we were much more flexible about the quality.

Let us take it one step further. Let us say that at your office there is a jar and for each time that a person is late, he is to deposit $5 into it. It fills with money all month long and finally at the end of the month there is $150 in it. Your boss notices that you are going out to lunch and asks you if you wouldn't mind buying a prize for the end of the month drawing with the $150. You are happy to do so.

You embark upon the journey with the $150 in your pocket and lo and behold, you spy a horrendous four foot tall green frog in the store window. Unable to resist the utterly useless gag gift, you purchase it and take it to the office storage room.

The office raffle is then held and they open the door and present the prize: the frog. Everybody has a good laugh and it is fun. You spent money that was not yours and you cared neither for the quality nor the price.

Your office party purchase is called a "third party purchase." It is the purchase of something you will not consume with money that is not yours.

By definition, all government purchases are third party purchases. They are purchases made with money that is not theirs and they are purchases made on behalf of someone else. So will there be waste? You bet your bottom dollar there will – plenty of it.

> *By definition, all government purchases are third party purchases.*

Again, that is why Abraham Lincoln said, "We want government to do only those things which we cannot do for ourselves." As we discussed earlier, we cannot defend ourselves. So will there be waste in the Department of Defense? Absolutely. There will be waste in anything government does. Therefore, we wisely limit what it does.

Nations that fail to limit third party purchasing - that is, government control of the money - witness the wealth of their countries dissipate. The more money that goes to the government, the more third party purchasing, the poorer the nation. Its is as predictable of a formula as is $E = MC^2$.

While many compassionate voters support candidates who favor the programs which tug on their heartstrings, they fail to recognize the equivalent tug on their purse strings. They simply misunderstand. Since they believe there is a limited amount of wealth (fundamental misunderstanding), they truly believe that the compassionate, caring thing to do is to elect the guy who favors government control (wrong conclusion). **To repeat, a fundamental failing in understanding will lead to wrong conclusions.** A pattern of such wrong conclusions will lead to greater government control, increased third party purchasing, and less freedom. It will suffocate the entrepreneur and deplete the wealth of any nation who follows it.

> *A fundamental failing in understanding will lead to wrong conclusions.*

GOVERNMENT EFFICIENCY

The Ten Commandments contain 297 words.

The Bill of Rights is stated in 463 words.

The Lord's prayer has only 67.

The story of creation in the Bible uses only 200 words.

Lincoln's Gettysburg Address contains 271 words.

On the other hand, a recent Federal directive to regulate the price of cabbage contains 26,911 words.

PRICE SIGNALS

Let us return to our principle: **the greater the freedom, the greater the wealth**. Another reason a free economy increases wealth and government control decreases wealth is because of price signals.

A price signal operates in a free market and tells you if your product is of good quality and if it is well-priced. Unlike an entrepreneur, whose success or failure depends largely on price signals, the government is not equipped to accept price signals.

Suppose there is a parade and everyone is out on the street. It is hot and you, the entrepreneur, see cokes for sale down the street for one dollar. You know all of the people along the parade route are hot and thirsty and you think that people will be willing to pay some money for those cokes. You therefore buy twenty of them for a dollar each and you then walk along the curb and try to sell them for four dollars. Nobody buys. You lower your price to three dollars. Still, no takers. Finally, you reduce your price to two dollars and people start to hand over their money. Why? It was worth it for them to not have to leave their chairs and to walk the distance to buy the coke at a cheaper price.

What happened? The price mechanism showed what was the proper price to charge. Since government is not susceptible to that mechanism, under Socialism the government does things over which you have no control. When you want to get your license plate, the government decides what it is going to charge and you have no choice: you must pay. Whether it is health care or housing, the government is not susceptible to price signals. As a result, they waste money and nations become poor.

> *Whether it is health care or housing, the government is not susceptible to price signals.*

THE ENTREPRENEUR

An entrepreneur is the person who accepts the risks and the responsibility for the operations of a business enterprise. It is the entrepreneurs who create wealth in a country. When government attempts to fairly distribute its country's wealth by increasing taxes and engaging in third party purchasing, it hinders and often eliminates the activities of entrepreneurs.

Let us consider the example of Mr. and Mrs. Free Enterprise. Mr. and Mrs. FE both work full-time and decide that they would like to increase their standard of living. After all, they live in a Free Enterprise system and are thus free to do so.

Since Mr. and Mrs. FE have not had a profitable partnership with Uncle Sam, they must borrow money to start their business. That is, they must **assume risk**. They develop a business plan according to which they must quit their jobs, solicit customers, maintain accounting, maintain equipment, and hire laborers.

For the latter, they decide to hire Joe College. He is on his summer vacation and is looking for a way to make some extra cash before returning to school.

Mr. and Mrs. FE determine that they must make enough profit to do five things:

1) Pay back their lenders;
2) Provide for raw materials e.g. gas and oil;
3) Pay their laborers;
4) Pay themselves so that they can continue to provide for their family; and
5) Set some profit aside into a seed corn account i.e. **capital account**, so that when the lawn mower wears out they can replace it.

The lawn mower is called a **tool of production** and is a **capital investment**. If Mr. and Mrs. FE work hard enough and put enough in their **capital account**, they can then buy a second mower and hire a second laborer.

This is a fundamental fact: the capital account is there for the sole purpose of replacing equipment. If they use the money for something else, they must pay income tax on it. If they use it to replace their worn out lawn mower, it is called a capital gain.

Who is allowed access to that account? Only two people. The first is Mr. Politician. He can pass a capital gains tax, which every year gets into that account and takes money away.

There is one other source that can access that account. Our friend Joe College is out mowing lawns and who should step out from behind the bushes but Mr. Union Organizer. He says, "Joe, you pay me $15 per week and I'll go negotiate your agreement with Mr. FE. Because, you know Joe, if it weren't for us, you wouldn't have this job."

Joe College says, "Oh! I thought it was because of Mr. FE that I had this job." "No, no," says Mr. Union Organizer, "if it weren't for the Lawnmower Union, you wouldn't have a job at all. Listen, Joe, you pay me $15 per week and I'll get you a raise." The prospect of a raise sounds good to Joe, and so he hands over his $15.

Mr. Union then goes to Mr. FE. "Mr. FE, I've looked over your books and see that you have money in that capital account and we believe our people deserve more." Mr. FE is astonished. "Your people! Your people? Where were you when Joe College was wandering up and down the street looking for a job?"

"Listen," says Mr. Union, "if you don't pay Joe an extra $10 per day and give him Fridays off, we'll quit working." Mr. FE thinks about this. "Well, then, we'll just hire someone else." "No, no, no," replies Mr. Union, "You can't do that. We got a law passed against you doing that. So, you make your decision by Sunday night or as of Monday, you'll be mowing lawns yourself." What happens? Mr. FE caves in to the coercive power of Mr. Union and takes money out of the capital account to pay Joe College $10 more per day.

This is a critical lesson in wealth creation. **Nations that want to create jobs protect capital gains and discourage capital gains tax.** That is why the capital gains tax in Japan, Hong Kong, Germany and South Korea are zero. In rich, smart countries the capital gains tax is zero and entrepreneurism thrives.

WORDS TO THE WISE

When a plague of poverty decimated an ancient land, the King called in his wisest economic advisors and demanded to be shown a short textbook on economics so that he might devise a remedy.

A full year later, the Kings advisors returned bearing not one but eighty-seven volumes. Enraged at having his order ignored, the King ordered his guards to execute half of the advisors.

Fearful for their lives, the remaining advisors culled the economics texts down to four volumes. To this , the angry King responded by ordering his guards to execute all but one of the remaining economic experts.

Finally, trembling, the last royal economist bowed before the King and said, " Sire, in five words I will reveal to all the wisdom that I have distilled through all the economists who once practiced their science in your kingdom."

"Quick," replied the impatient King. "What is it?" Answered the counselor, "There ain't no free lunch"

GOVERNMENT BEHAVES EXACTLY THE OPPOSITE OF FREE ENTERPRISE

Mr. and Mrs. FE were willing to assume the risk of business ownership because they understood this principle: **the greater the contribution, the greater the reward**. They understood that in a free market, they could increase their standard of living by increasing their contribution.

In a free market, a brain surgeon receives a greater financial reward than does an elevator operator because the brain surgeon contributes a more valuable service.

It follows that in a free market, a person is rewarded for good behavior and punished for bad behavior. If an entrepreneur gives people a good cup of coffee at a good price, they will reward him by frequenting his store and contributing to its success. If he gives a rotten cup of coffee at a rotten price, the next week the coffee bar will be out of business.

All government operates on the opposite scale. Government rewards bad behavior and punishes good behavior. If you choose to get married, have a job and have a child, the government will punish you by taking money away from you in the form of taxing that behavior. If you choose to not get married, not get a job, and have a child, the government will reward you by giving you housing, food and medical care.

Again, if you fix up your house - paint it, mow the lawn, plant shrubbery – your house's value increases. What does the government do? It places a higher tax burden on your home. However, if you let your home fall apart, the government will reward you with lower taxes.

The reason that America is the richest nation on earth is because it does less of that than any other nation. Ludwig von Meses, from Austria, said, "In America, they have the highest standard of living because the government of that nation embarked later than the government of other nations upon a program of interfering with free enterprise."

Since government behaves exactly the opposite of Free Enterprise, it is no surprise that Socialism has been an utter failure. It has never, ever worked. Not in any country, not at any time.

While the Soviet Union was intact, it was number two in gold in the world, yet it was in total abject poverty. Hong Kong is literally built on a rock. It has absolutely no natural resources. Yet because it was under British Colonial Rule for 155 years before its recent return to China, its economy developed under a free system. As a result, its output per person is forty times as great as China. Likewise, West Germany had a standard of living ten times as high as East Germany, even though the two shared the same language, the same culture, the same climate.

Free Enterprise, on the other hand, is the natural order of things. It has proven itself successful in nations throughout history. Why? Because when there is a need to be filled, there is no government restriction. When there is a need to be filled, an entrepreneur, a risk taker, a private individual, will seek to fulfill that gap. In the process, wealth proliferates.

We must recognize that when we restrict an individual's ability to create, we take a giant step towards Socialism. It is for this reason that economics are such a vital ingredient in the political P.I.E.

CHAPTER THREE: INTEGRITY

"WHY DOES INTEGRITY MATTER?"

Principle: If a person does what is wrong, then he will not do what is right.

Impact: Our choice of any important partner, business or political, requires the vital ingredient of Integrity in order to be trusted.

Explanation: When we choose political leaders, we are electing people to represent our values and interests. We elect them to do the things that we would like to see done.

But how do we know that what we want, and what they will do, will coincide? The answer is found in one word: Integrity.

Webster defines integrity as meaning soundness, reliability. You think of a structure that has integrity as being solid. You can put your trust in it.

Perhaps the most revered President in our history was George Washington. Unanimously elected, George Washington embodied integrity. As Benjamin Franklin said of him, "He errs, as other men do, but he errs with integrity."

While we know what integrity of a structure is, what is integrity in a person? It is two things. Morality and Character.

Morality is refraining from doing what is wrong.

Character is doing what is right.

The Ten Commandments are the most widely accepted standard of Morality. "Thou shalt not steal, thou shalt not bear false witness (lie), thou shalt not commit adultery." Morality governs the basic standards of a civilized society. Contracts are honored because the person signing them has given his word, and will not lie. It is the short hand foundation of all successful economies and governments.

Character includes and goes beyond morality. Character is doing what is right. Suppose your daughter comes home from school and reports that the other children in her class were picking on Sally. They made fun of her appearance or her weight or her speech. Your daughter then says proudly, "but I didn't do it."

Naturally it is good that she did not do anything wrong. Her direct actions, in and of themselves, were not immoral. But, did she have the character to do what was right? Did she protect or defend her abused classmate to the degree she was able?

> *Integrity consists of Morality, not doing what is wrong, and Character, doing what is right.*

Thus, Integrity consists of both Morality, not doing what is wrong, and Character, doing what is right. People operating under this standard can be relied upon. They can be trusted. They have Integrity.

You can turn your back and feel confident that, even when you are not looking, they will do what is right.

This is at odds with those who are merely Moral. That is they are principled enough to not do things that are wrong, or illegal. But, on the other hand, you cannot rely upon them to do what is right when the times are difficult. On such occasions they wilt into

---

"I WILL"

The Greek sculptor, Phidias, had high standards when he was carving the statue of Athenia for the Acropolis.

He was busy chiseling the strands of her hair at the back of her head when an onlooker commented, "That figure is to stand 100 feet high, with its back to a marble wall. Who will ever know what details you are putting behind there?"

Phidias replied, "I will."

---

the shadows and cannot be counted upon to stand firm. As Abraham Lincoln so aptly stated, "To sin by silence when they should protest makes cowards out of men."

They are not doing anything wrong, but neither are they doing what is right. Perhaps all of us have had the occasion to be disappointed when someone we admired lacked the character to do what was right.

Logically one can see that one must first be moral in order to be a person of character. **Simply put, by definition if a person is doing what is wrong (immoral) he cannot do what is right (character).**

That is why many Americans were left scratching their heads when defenders of the immoral activities of former President Clinton would say things similar to the statement by former New York governor Mario Cuomo to the effect that, "I would not trust him with my sister, but I would trust him with the nation's secrets".

Many Americans found it profoundly confusing

that a person who could not be trusted because he did wrong things, would nevertheless in matters of politics do what was right.

Any parent that upon discovering that her daughter is dating a repeatedly convicted thief would take little solace in the statement, "but Mom, he doesn't steal from me." The fact that he does what is wrong preempts our capacity to expect that, in time of stress, he would do what is right. **In other words, he lacks integrity.** His lack of morality (doing what is wrong) precludes his being relied upon to do what is right (character).

Our choice of any important partner, business or political, requires the vital ingredient of Integrity in order to be trusted.

Unfortunately, however, history tends to lead us to the conclusion that Economy is more important than Integrity. The election of Hitler in Germany is a perfect example. He improved the economy in Germany, but he was lacking in Integrity. Disaster resulted.

This is true even when the electorate is fully aware of the lack of integrity. The choice is often "It's the economy, stupid" that trumps the question of Integrity.

That should not deter us, however, from establishing as the standard for secure political leadership the well balanced combination of both Integrity and Economics. Without them both, we will surely watch our nation crumble.

CHAPTER FOUR:
OUR HISTORY,
OUR LEGACY

It was August 24, 1814. The First Lady of the Land Dolly Madison was preparing a spread for lunch for her husband President James Madison and his commanders. Just as the table spread was being completed, a military messenger came rushing into the White House to report that President Madison would not be coming for lunch, but that the British were.

Five days earlier, the British had entered Chesapeake Bay and had begun their attack on Washington. Now they were entering the burning city. President Madison, the last President to command troops in the field, had commanded a portion of the city's defenses. Since he was not going to make it back to the White House, a messenger had been sent to warn the President's family and staff that they too were about to be overrun.

Dolly had only moments to escape. She chose to take just two things with her. She tore out the full-length oil portrait of George Washington that had been painted by Gilbert Stuart, and the portrait of herself that she had recently received. These were rolled and delivered to her carriage as the staff beat a hasty departure.

Moments later, the British soldiers entered the White House, ate the lunch prepared for the President and proceeded to enjoy the amenities of the mansion until nightfall. Then they "laid the torch to it," as had been done to the rest of the city. The great house, so lovingly procured by George Washington and inhabited by every President since Adams, was destroyed with none but the four fire scorched stone walls surviving.

The present White House carries only three artifacts form the period prior to this day. The Gilbert Stuart painting of General George Washington. Now hangs in the East Room of the reconstructed home. The portrait of Dolly Madison with its red backdrop is currently used to identify the shade of red that covers the red room in the White House, where her likeness now hangs. There is also the Adams' silver service today seen in the Green Room

And finally, during the 1989 repairs to the outside of the White House, the several layers of white paint were removed down to the stone. On the Truman Balcony chose to leave the area under one of the windowsills unpainted, in order that visitors could see the charred markings and be reminded of this day.

As the British continued to sack and burn the city, the flames from the blazing Capitol Building could be seen in the nation's third largest city, Baltimore, 40 miles away

The war had broken out in 1812 over Britain's attempts to regulate American shipping and dictate other activities to the young United States while

Britain was at war with France. As the ruler of the seas, the British Navy believed themselves free to steal (impress) sailors onto their warships if they felt they had need. The independence minded United States was willing to endure war rather than submit to such oppression.

While the British soldiers were withdrawing from Washington they took as a prisoner of war Dr. William Beanes, who resided in the nearby town of Upper Malboro. Dr. Beanes was much revered in the area, and was a friend of the young Washington lawyer Francis Scott Key.

The townsfolk of Upper Marlboro asked the talented Mr. Key to petition the British for return of Dr. Beanes, fearful that otherwise he would be hanged.

Learning that the doctor was being held on the British flagship, Key asked permission of the President to negotiate with the British for his return. President Madison approved the mission and sent along Colonel John Skinner as an official American agent for prisoner exchange.

On the morning of September 3rd, Francis and Col. Skinner set sail from Baltimore harbor to meet the British fleet, flying a flag of truce. They found and boarded the flagship Tonnant to confer with General Ross and Admiral Alexander Cochrane.

At first, the commanders refused to release Dr. Beanes. But Key and Skinner produced a pouch of letters written by wounded British prisoners, praising the care they were receiving from the Americans, particularly Dr. Beanes.

Finally the British officers relented, but would not release the three Americans immediately, fearing that they had seen and heard too much of the preparations for the attack on Baltimore. So, they were placed under guard and told that they would have to wait out the battle behind the British fleet.

Now let's go back for a moment a year earlier to the summer of 1813.

Americans knew that if they refused to capitulate to the various demands of the British, that Britain would again invade and attack our young country.

Fort McHenry was the star shaped military pro-
tection overlooking Baltimore harbor, America's
busiest seaport. Its commander, Major George
Armistead, felt confident that if the Americans did
not capitulate to the British, that they would assured-
ly attack his country. And when they did attack,
Major Armistead was certain that Fort McHenry
would be in the middle of the battle.

So, in anticipation of the coming struggle, he
ordered a flag so big that "the British will have no
trouble seeing it from a distance."

Two officers were sent to the Baltimore home of
Mary Young Pickersgill, a "maker of colors," and
commissioned a flag large enough to meet the Commander's needs.

Mary and her 13 year old daughter, Caroline,
immediately went to work, using 400 yards of the
best quality wool bunting. They cut 15 stars that
measured two feet from point to point. Eight red and
seven white stripes each two feet wide. By August,
the banner was finished. It measured 42 feet by 30
feet and cost $405.90.

Now, back to the following year and the three Americans leaning on the ramparts of the ship where they were under guard.

At 7 a.m. on the morning of September 13, 1814, the British bombardment of Fort McHenry began, and the flag was ready to meet the enemy. The bombardment continued all day and all night. The British fired 1,500 bombshells that weighed as much as 220 pounds and carried lighted fuses that were supposed to explode when they reached their target. However, they weren't always dependable and would often blow up in mid-air.

From special small boats, the British also fired new Congreve rockets that would trace a wobbly arc of red flame across the sky.

Now hear this.

The Americans, not soldiers, not sailors, just Americans had sunk 22 of their own vessels in the entrance to the harbor. This made a close approach by the British fleet impossible.

That evening the shelling stopped. This was a great source of concern for Key and the other Americans trapped in the midst of the British warships. Then around 1 AM on the 14th, the fleet again roared to life, lighting the rainy night sky with its grotesque fireworks.

Francis Scott Key, Col. Skinner and Dr. Beanes stood at the ramparts and watched the battle with apprehension. They knew that as long as the shelling continued, Fort McHenry had not surrendered. But, long before daylight, there came a sudden and mysterious silence once again. What they did not know was that the British assault on Baltimore, as well as the naval attack, had been abandoned. The same patriots that had sunk their own vessels in the harbor entrance had then positioned themselves in the lowlands where the enemy would be forced to land its troops. Giving the invading forces a greater opposition than they could handle, the British officers ordered a retreat.

In the predawn darkness, Key waited for the sight that would end his anxiety; the joyous sight of Major Armistead's great flag blowing in the breeze.

When at last by the early light of dawn, they could begin to make out that indeed, Our flag was still there!!

Being an amateur poet and hymn composer, and feeling uniquely inspired, Key began to write on the back of a letter he had in his packet.

Oh, say can you see,
by the dawn's early light,

What so proudly we hailed
at the twilight's last gleaming?

Whose broad stripes and bright stars,
through the perilous fight,

O'er the ramparts we watched,
were so gallantly streaming?

And the rockets' red glare,
the bombs bursting in air,

Gave proof through the night
that our flag was still there.

O say, does that star-spangled banner yet wave
O'er the land of the free and the home of the brave?

Sailing back to Baltimore, he composed more lines, and in his room at the Indian Queen Hotel he finished the poem.

Oh! thus be it ever,
when freemen shall stand

Between their loved homes
and the war's desolation!

Blest with victory and peace,
may the heaven-rescued land

Praise the Power that hath made
and preserved us a nation.

Then conquer we must,
when our cause it is just,

And this be our motto:
"In God is our trust."

And the star-spangled banner in triumph shall wave
O'er the land of the free and the home of the brave!

* * *

Let us conclude with some final thoughts on this country of ours – this land of the free and the home of the brave. As President George W. Bush has said, "our greatest export to the world has been, is, and always will be the incredible freedom we understand in America."

America. It is the place to which people hope to someday escape. It is the lighthouse of freedom. It is the place where people know that if they can just get under the shadow of the flag, they will be okay.

You have what the rest of the world prays to someday have. Its future is in your hands.